INDOOR CANNABIS GROWING

A QUICK GUIDE TO GROWING CANNABIS INDOORS

BAILEY YATES

Table of Contents

CHAPTER ONE 3

INDOOR CANNABIS GROWING 3

Indoor Cannabis Planting 3

The first step is to deal with the setup. 4

CHAPTER TWO 12

Supply CO2 to the atmosphere. 20

CHAPTER THREE 24

Grow lights should be put in place. 24

Determine how much light you need. 25

CHAPTER THREE 32

Follow these steps to keep tabs on your plants' growth and make necessary lighting adjustments: 37

CHAPTER FOUR 42

A watering and fertilization system must be chosen. 43

Maintain a spotless grow space. 52

CHAPTER ONE

INDOOR CANNABIS GROWING

Indoor Cannabis Planting

It's not like growing a houseplant when it comes to cultivating cannabis. With a grow room, you'll have more control over everything from the lighting to the air circulation to the temperature and humidity. A grow room is a necessity if you're growing photoperiod plants, which need 12 hours of darkness per day during the flowering stage.

An empty bedroom or closet will do just fine as your first storage space. Put up a grow tent (or grow box) in an area of your home, basement, or garage if you don't have a suitable room. A grow tent can be purchased or made from scratch. The following must be included in your grow space or tent:

• Enough room to accommodate the number of plants and their sizes that you intend to cultivate. This includes making sure that the space is tall enough to accommodate the plant's height, and that the grow light is hung high enough to avoid burning the plant. One or two plants can be grown in a three-foot-square, six-foot-tall space.

• Lightproof. The walls should be impermeable to light from the outside. The room should be completely dark if you shut the door during the day or when the lights in the area are on. (Autoflowering strains don't need to worry about this as much.)

Walls, floors, and ceilings painted white or reflectively. It's a waste of light if the interior isn't reflecting it; otherwise, it's absorbing it. There should be no shadows, so that your plants can soak up as much light as possible.

• Waterproof tray or drain on the floor. You'll need a way to collect any plant waste that leaks out.

• Ventilation fan openings There must be at least two openings in the room, typically one at the bottom and one at the top of each end.

Additionally, there should be a place for the power cords and other electrical components.

Grow lights and other equipment will need to be hung from some sort of framework at the very top.

Accurately mimic the desired weather.

It's all up to Mother Nature when you're growing outside. That's what you do when you're growing indoors. Temperature, humidity, and airflow all play a role in climate control. Each stage of development necessitates a unique set of ideal conditions.

Warm and moist conditions are necessary for seed germination in the dark. In a mini greenhouse, you can start seeds in moistened soil plugs (available at most hardware stores). Keep an eye on the seeds to make sure they don't dry out.

- Seedling/vegetative: Maintain a temperature of 75-80 degrees Fahrenheit and a relative humidity of 60-70 percent while in the vegetative stage. Outside air is needed to help cool your room and deliver a steady supply of carbon dioxide, so make sure you have adequate ventilation in place (CO2). Between 700 and 900 parts per million of CO2 should be present in the atmosphere (ppm). In order to maintain the health of the plants, proper circulation is required.

•	Flowering: Maintain a temperature of 72-78 degrees Fahrenheit and a relative humidity of 50-55 percent during the flowering stage. The buds are less susceptible to fungal infection if the humidity level is reduced. There should be no more than 1,500 parts per million of CO_2 in the atmosphere at all times (ppm).

Never go below 60 degrees Fahrenheit or above 85 degrees

Fahrenheit in terms of temperature.

Focus your attention on the movement of the air around you

Outdoor plant cultivation encourages air circulation around the plants. Plants need adequate ventilation and circulation when grown indoors. While ventilation brings fresh air into the room, circulation circulates air within the room. Plants benefit from ventilation and circulation in a variety of ways, including the following:

CHAPTER TWO

Increased humidity in the grow room is a result of the heat generated by the grow lights. In a grow room, an exhaust fan removes hot and humid air, creating a vacuum that attracts cooler and drier air (assuming the room has intake holes or vents).

• Provide plants with CO_2 (O_2). If the CO_2 supply in the room isn't replenished, the plants "suffocate" and die.

Pests and diseases can be prevented by preventing mold,

mildew, fungi and certain pests from flourishing in warm, humid, stagnant air. This problem can be solved by bringing in cooler, drier air, and having a breeze in the room helps to discourage gnat infestations.

Increase the sturdiness of plant stems and leaves: Plants that are exposed to a breeze become more robust, which in turn helps flower buds to flourish.

Grow room air flow is the most common cause of crop failure and reduced yields.

Make sure there is enough air flow.

The first step is to install an exhaust fan or an intake fan, or both, to ventilate the room. An active ventilation system consists of a large exhaust fan on one end of the room and a smaller intake fan on the other. You only need one fan in a passive system. One or more holes in the opposite end of the room are used to bring in or remove air from the room when the exhaust fan or intake fan is operating. When using a passive cooling system, the hole (or holes) without the fan must be larger.

For the most part, grow rooms make use of the low-tech but effective in-line duct fans that can be installed in minutes. For the most part, it's the same as connecting a dryer to a flexible duct pipe. Depending on the size of the room and the size of any existing holes, you can purchase in-line duct fans with a diameter of 4, 6, or 8 inches. The most common size of ceiling fan is six inches in diameter. Buy fans to match the size of the ventilation holes in your grow tent.

In addition, look into the fan's cubic feet per minute (CFM) rating, and purchase a fan whose CFM rating is higher than the room's cubic feet volume. There should be enough ventilation in a grow room so that the air can be completely replaced once every minute. Take the length, width, and height of the room in feet and multiply them together to get the total square footage. A fan rated at 100 CFM would be adequate in a room that is 3-by-3-by-6 feet in size, for example. However, if you're pumping air over a long distance or the duct pipe has several bends, you may require a fan with a higher CFM rating.

Your intake hole should be at the bottom of the room and your exhaust hole should be at the top. Because heat naturally rises to the top, the exhaust hole is elevated.

Install a filter on the intake and exhaust ducts whether you're using one or two fans. To prevent bugs, mold spores from contaminating the water supply, the intake filter is used. In most cases, the exhaust filter is a carbon filter that aids in the reduction of cannabis-related odors as they leave the room. Filters can be attached to fans directly or through the use of a flexible duct pipe.

Use the smallest amount of duct pipe possible and run it as straight as possible. More bends and a longer distance to travel mean less efficient air flow in a pipe Use fans with higher CFM ratings if you must run pipe a long distance or make a bend.

Move the air around in a circling motion.

It's also critical to have good air flow. In respiration, plants do not "exhale" with any kind of force, as is the case with animals. Carbon dioxide (CO_2) can be breathed in by plants by using fans to circulate the air, which removes the oxygen (O_2) surrounding them. Your grow room needs at least one fan to keep the air flowing properly. Choosing how many fans to use and where to put them in the room is largely a matter of trial and error. It's a goal to have every part of the plant "dancing"—every leaf should be gently shaking. A fan may need to be moved or an additional fan added if you notice any part of the plant that isn't dancing.

Start with two small fans in opposite corners of the room or one slightly larger oscillating fan in one corner of the room, and then make adjustments as you go along.

Supply CO_2 to the atmosphere.

CO2 is essential for plant life. This is an example of the mutually beneficial relationship between plants and animals. All living things take in CO2 and exhale it, but plants do the opposite. Although CO2 sublimation is not required if your grow room has adequate air flow and you're using high intensity lighting, it does increase overall yields.

CO2 can be added to a grow room in a variety of ways. A CO2 tank can be purchased and pumped into the room, or dry ice or CO2 canisters and bags can be purchased that slowly release the gas into the room over time. Keep these things in mind if you're going to be adding CO2 to your grow room:

• Do not add CO2 unless the lights are already on. During the day, plants use CO2 at a much slower rate, so any CO2 added during the night is CO2 as well.

In order to avoid pumping the gas out and wasting it, turn off the intake and exhaust fans for a few minutes before releasing CO2.

CO2 should be added from the top of the room and in front of one of your circulating fans. Because it has a higher density than air, it tends to fall to the ground. Using a CO2 tank as an example, run a hose up to the grow room's ceiling and place it in front of a fan.

To keep CO2 levels at 900 ppm during the vegetative stage and 1,150 ppm during flowering, use a CO2 meter. To measure CO2, you'll need a CO2 meter.

CHAPTER THREE

In order for the plant to take advantage of the increased light intensity, additional CO_2 is required.

An indoor grow's success is directly related to the quality of its lighting. Lights, how they're set up, and other equipment that controls and directs them are the most important factors in determining your final product's yield and flavor. Grow light selection and installation are explained in detail here.

Determine how much light you need.

Decide how much light your plants require before you head to the nursery or hardware store to look for grow lights. Depending on the strain, a standard 1,000-watt grow light should be able to accommodate four plants with a fully grown diameter of approximately 3 feet. As soon as you've set up your grow lights and plants, you'll want to check to see if any of the plants are getting enough light.

Lighting fixtures and bulbs can The majority of standard light fixtures and bulbs in the average home are insufficient for cannabis cultivation. They don't give plants the quality and quantity of light they require to thrive. Although T5 and CFL bulbs are acceptable, they produce smaller, lower-quality buds than other lighting options. Fluorescent lighting is not recommended by us.

Having ruled out fluorescent lighting as an option, the next step is to decide on the type of grow light that will best serve your needs.

It is best to use high intensity discharge (HID) bulbs in the vegetative and flowering stages if you want high yields. MH bulbs are best in the vegetative stage and HPS bulbs in the flowering stage. Because of how much light and heat these bulbs produce, you should place them further away from the plants.

- If you want to extract more terpenes, use LED or ceramic metal halide (CMH) bulbs instead of high-intensity discharge (HID) lighting because these bulbs preserve the terpenes without increasing the flower weight and density.

Lighting fixtures are determined by the bulbs you plan on using. Shop for a grow light system that includes all of the lighting components you require, including the bulbs, after you've selected a bulb type. Grow room lighting includes the following components and features:

With a reflector hood, you can direct light down to your plants from a light fixture. Reflector hoods are available in a variety of styles, including:

closed hood: This type of reflector is shaped like a box and produces a more focused beam of light (and heat).

There are openings on the ends of the vents, which allow the hood to be connected to in-line duct fans for cooling.

Closed-hood reflectors focus light more tightly than those with wings, which are made of curved and texturized aluminum sheets. The light spreads out over a larger area, but the intensity is lower (so is the heat).

Light is dispersed in a circular pattern by a parabolic hood, which has an umbrella-like shape.

There is no right or wrong answer when it comes to hoods. If you're worried about the heat, opt for a hooded design;

otherwise, go with a wing or parabolic shape.

In order to keep the lightbulb from overheating, a ballast limits how much current it draws from the power source. In general, there are two kinds of ballasts:

• Magnetic: Less expensive, heavy, hot, noisy, flicker-prone and only supports bulbs of a certain wattage are some of the drawbacks of this option. It's necessary to replace the ballast if you want to switch from 400W to 600W bulbs, for example.

CHAPTER THREE

A dimmable option may be available for digital lights but they are more expensive, less efficient, less susceptible to flicker, cooler, quieter, and less prone to radio frequency interference than their analogue counterparts.

Hanging light fixtures in your grow room often necessitates the use of hooks and pulleys, which are included in many grow light systems. It is much easier to raise and lower light fixtures with the aid of pulleys so that they are at the proper height from the tops of the plants.

Using a timer to automate the process of turning on and off your grow lights is available as an add-on feature or as a stand-alone purchase.

So, how do you do that?

To ensure an even distribution of light, mount the light fixtures to the ceiling of your grow room above your plants. The type of fixture you use and the layout of your grow room's ceiling will determine how you install the light fixtures. It's possible to hang your fixtures in such a way that you can easily raise or lower them to the proper distance from the tops of your plants using hooks, chains, or even pulleys.

Place the lights so that they shine directly on the plants, illuminating every inch of each one. As close as possible without burning the highest part of the plant should be used for lighting. When adjusting the lights, keep an eye on the plants and raise the light if the tops of any plants are getting burned.

Don't expose anything flammable to the light in such a way that it could be ignited by the light.

Adjust the timers.

Plants require 18 to 24 hours of light per day while in the vegetative stage. There must be at least 12 hours of total darkness during the flowering/blooming stage for photoperiod strains and 10 to 12 hours of light during this time period for auto-flowering strains. Using timers for your grow lights makes it much easier to keep track of the necessary light/dark cycles, but you'll still need to keep track of how the lighting changes throughout the growth cycle.

For a garden where some plants are growing and others are blooming, you'll need to adjust your lighting accordingly. Plants in the vegetative and flowering stages of the photoperiod cycle should be grown in separate tents or rooms.

The vegetative stage requires that the lights be placed at the correct distance above the canopy.

You should set your light timers to provide light for between 18 and 24 hours. To find the ideal amount of light for each strain, experiment with a variety of settings in that range over a number of grows.

To keep the lights at the proper distance from your plants' tops as they grow taller, watch your plants and make any necessary lighting adjustments.

Your plants are ready to transition from the vegetative stage to the flower stage when they are about half the size of full-grown plants. (You can either adjust the lighting or move the plants to the flower tent or room at this point).

Light, container size, and other environmental factors such as CO2 can all affect a plant's final growth size. You may need to grow a strain multiple times to get a clear picture of what a mature plant looks like and when it's ready to transition from the vegetative to flowering stages.

Use HPS bulbs for flowering if you used MH bulbs during the vegetative stage.

Replace fluorescent, CFL or LED bulbs if you want to save money on your electricity bill.

During the first few days of using the brighter HPS bulbs,

cover the plants with a tarp to protect them from the intense light. Use a piece of cardboard to separate the light from the plants, but keep it as far away from the bulb as possible to avoid a fire.

Make sure your lights are at the right height for the flowering stage by adjusting their height.

A minimum of 12 hours of darkness and 10–12 hours of light should be provided to the plants by setting the timers. Try a variety of lighting conditions between grows to see which works best for your auto-flowering strains. They don't require 12 hours of darkness.

During the flowering stage, keep an eye on your plants and adjust the light height as necessary to maintain the proper distance from the plants' tops. You know your plant is ready to be harvested when half of the buds turn orange and red in color.

CHAPTER FOUR

Calculate the amount of light there is.

The yield is strongly influenced by the brightness of the light. As close as possible to the plants, but not so close as to burn them, the lights should be placed. Raise the lights if the tops of any plants are wilting or burning.

Obtain a photosynthetic active radiation (PAR) meter and measure the light's PAR output at various locations above the canopy for more advanced grows. There should never be a PAR reading above 1,200.

A watering and fertilization system must be chosen.

Your plants need a watering and fertilizing system, no matter if you're growing them indoors or out. Manual or automatic are your only real choices. First-time growers are advised to use a manual method to learn how much water and fertilizer they need.

Consider installing an automated irrigation system after learning about your plants' water and nutrient requirements, which may vary depending on the strain. Using timers, these devices water and feed plants on a predetermined schedule. Automated lighting systems have the same advantages as lighting systems, such as ease of use and reliability. You must, however, continue to keep an eye on your plants to ensure that they receive an appropriate amount of water and nutrition.

Make use of a hydroponic system.

As a rule, plants are grown in non-soil-based growing media like pea gravel, expanded clay aggregate, coco coir or vermiculite in hydroponic systems. Water and nutrients are then delivered to the roots via a variety of systems (illustrated in Figure 11-1):

• Aeroponic: Roots dangle from a tray suspended above a water/nutrient reservoir in this method. Every few minutes, water from the reservoir is sprayed onto the roots, where it drips back into the reservoir.

Nutrient-rich water is slowly dripped into the growing medium and absorbed by the roots through a drip system. A waste reservoir collects and eventually disposes of any remaining water.

As the name suggests, deep water culture (DWC) involves placing plants in baskets above an aerated (and typically chilled) water/nutrient reservoir with their roots submerged in the solution. This allows for continuous feeding.

• Ebb and flow: Plants sit in pots on a grow tray in an ebb and flow fashion. A constant supply of nutrient-rich water is pumped into the growing tray, where it is distributed to the pots through holes in the bottom and sides. The pumping is halted and the water is allowed to return to the reservoir from which it was drawn.

There are two types of NFT: ebb and flow, and nutrient film technique (NFT). A grow tray sits on top of baskets containing plants. A reservoir filled with nutrient-rich water is constantly pumped into the grow tray and then drained back into the reservoir. This setup ensures that the roots receive a steady supply of nutrient-rich water.

As the plant grows, an absorbent material (such as felt or rope) is placed through the middle of the growth medium into the reservoir, which is aerated and nutrient-rich. It's possible to give plants as much or as little water and nutrients as they need because of capillary action.

You can increase your chances of a successful hydroponics grow by following these tips:

• Use isopropyl alcohol or bleach to disinfect all of your hydroponics equipment in between growing cycles to kill any bacteria or infectious agents. In filthy systems, anaerobic bacteria can build up and eventually kill your plants.

• Use water that is free of impurities and has a neutral pH. Distilled water or reverse osmosis water can be used.

• Aerate the water solution rich in nutrients. You can use a small air pump from a pet store to aerate the reservoir by placing an aeration stone in the bottom. Your plants may not get the oxygen they need if you don't aerate them.

Water and nutrients should be replaced every two weeks. To avoid overdosing on nutrients, don't simply add them to your diet. For the vegetative stage, use a nitrogen-rich fertilizer, while for the flowering stage, use one with higher potassium and phosphorous concentrations.)

For disinfection, flush the system with dilute water and hydrogen peroxide solution, followed by plain water, after discarding the old nutrient mixture.

Every time the solution of nutrients is changed, consider flushing the growing medium with plain water.

You should do some research before purchasing and installing a hydroponics system to determine which system is best for your growing space and your level of expertise. Sometimes, less is more. Before you begin growing, make sure your system is leak-free and constructed with high-quality food-grade plastics.

Keep your grow room tidy, even if it means sounding like your mother. Bacteria, fungi, and pests thrive in a stale, unsanitary environment in a grow room. Keep your grow room clean by following these tips:.

Wash and disinfect plant containers and trays after each use; this includes irrigation hoses and pumps. Then follow up with isopropyl alcohol or bleach solution and soap and water (one part bleach to three parts water). Then, use a hose to rinse everything thoroughly.

• Make sure your grow room is free of dead plant material and other debris. In a healthy garden, this is where many pests and pathogens can get a foothold.

There are many different kinds of insects you should be on the lookout for when it comes to pest control. If you spot even one of these pests, identify it and find a pesticide that works. Fortunately, you can always rely on the helpful staff at your local nursery or garden center for assistance with this.